The MOST IMPORTANT ANIMAL of ALL

Written by Penny Worms

Illustrated by Hannah Bailey

With thanks to consultants Alex Morss;
Gemma Bailey, The Big Cat Sanctuary; Dr. Ali
Birkett and Dr. Sally Keith, Lancaster University;
Professor Helen Roy, UK Centre for Ecology and
Hydrology; and Dr. Christopher Jeffs,
British Ecological Society.

First published in the UK in 2021 by Mama Makes Books
Copyright © 2021 Mama Makes Books Ltd • Artwork © 2021 Hannah Bailey • Photos © page 40
Published in the United States by Jolly Fish Press, an imprint of North Star Editions, Inc.
First US Edition • First US Printing, 2023
ISBN 978-1-63163-701-8
Printed in the United States of America
Cataloging-in-Publication Data is on record at the Library of Congress

It was the first day of school. The children walked into the classroom, and everything was different. There was a jungle where the book corner used to be, an ocean instead of a mat, and huge butterflies on the ceiling.

"Children," the teacher said, "we are going to learn all about animals. Big ones, small ones, tiny ones. We will discover amazing things, and at the end of the semester, I'd like you to decide which animal is the most important of them all."

Their teacher was right. They did learn amazing things.
They learned how caterpillars turn into butterflies...

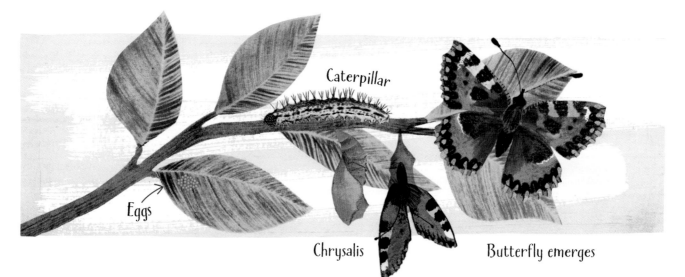

Caterpillar

Eggs

Chrysalis

Butterfly emerges

how fish breathe in water...

Gills

Water goes
in its mouth
with oxygen

Water comes
out of its gills

and why penguins are birds but cannot fly.

Penguins have evolved*
to "fly" through water
to catch fish.

* see glossary on page 39

At the end of the semester, the teacher said, "So children, who would like to share their ideas for which is the most important animal of all?"

George's hand shot up, and this is what he said.
"I think the most important animal of all is..."

ELEPHANTS

"Do you know the main difference between an African and Asian elephant?" asked George. "African elephants are huge! They are the biggest land animals on Earth.

"Both have a trunk, which is a nose, a hose, and a hand rolled into one. They use it to put food and water into their mouths. They suck up water for a shower and smell with it too."

African elephants have larger ears . . .

African elephant

. . . and they all grow tusks.

Asian elephant

Only some Asian males have tusks.

6

"But what makes elephants important is that they help all the other animals and plants around them survive and thrive."

Elephants are smart and have amazing memories. When there is no rain, they remember where there is water and use their tusks, trunks, and feet to dig for it.

They make these watering holes bigger when they bathe and cool themselves.

When the elephants leave, other animals can enjoy the water.

Thank you, elephants!

But George hadn't finished ...

He showed some photos.
"In the jungle," he said, "elephants create pathways that other animals and people use. They also help new plants grow by pulling down branches and letting sunlight through to the forest floor."

"Even their poo is useful!" George explained.

People use it to keep mosquitoes away, to enrich the soil, to build homes, and to burn like logs on a fire. They make paper out of it too.

The dung is full of seeds from the fruit the elephants eat. The seeds begin to grow, creating new plants.

Insects love elephant poo! Dung beetles eat it. Females lay their eggs in it so that when the babies hatch, they have a tasty poo breakfast. Some dung beetles roll balls of it away with an egg inside so no one steals it!

George smiled. "You see, elephants are important to trees, plants, animals, and people, so the elephant must be the most important animal of all."
Nimmie's arm went up. She had another animal in mind...

BEES

"Bees are little animals that make a BIG difference. They help new flowers grow and help produce a lot of the foods we eat.

"Not all the bees we see buzzing around are honeybees that live in huge colonies with a queen. Big, hairy bumblebees live in small colonies. Solitary bees, like the mason bee, live alone. But they all go from flower to flower searching for food."

"When a bee visits a flower, it drinks up the nectar, a sweet juice the flower produces. It also collects a yellow dust called pollen as food for baby bees."

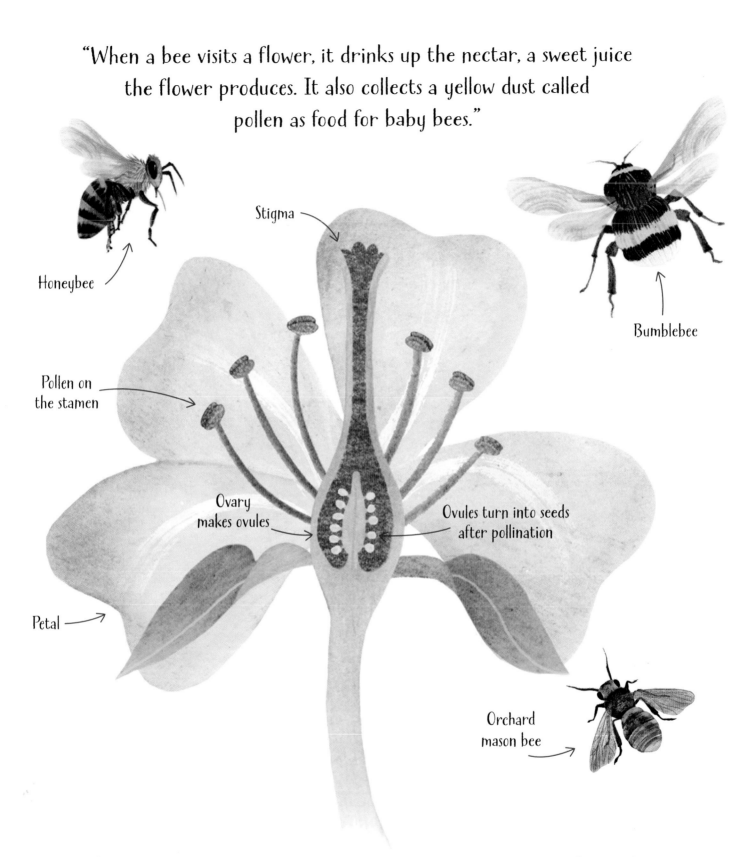

Honeybee

Stigma

Bumblebee

Pollen on the stamen

Ovary makes ovules

Ovules turn into seeds after pollination

Petal

Orchard mason bee

"When a bee flies to another flower, some pollen sticks to the stigma on the new flower. This is called pollination. Many plants need this to happen so they can grow fruits and seeds."

Pollen sticks
to a bee's
hairs.

Pollen basket
to take back
to the hive

Nimmie showed the class her photos.
"Farmers keep beehives in their
orchards and fields. These bees join
the wild bees that live around the
farm. All the bees are happy because
there is lots of food. The farmers are
happy because the bees pollinate
some of their crops and fruit trees."

"Bees are like fairies for farmers," she said.
"They pollinate their crops for free!"

Bees make honey, but they also help
produce fruits, vegetables, nuts, oils,
and some herbs and spices.

Wild bees don't live in hives.
They live in nests or build
combs like this one.

Bees and other pollinators,* such as beetles
and butterflies, pollinate wildflowers and trees,
providing food and shelter for other wild animals.

"Everyone needs bees!" Nimmie concluded.
"That's why the bee is the most important animal of all."
The class clapped for Nimmie's bees, but Seb had another animal in mind . . .

Whale shark

SHARKS

"Did you know that sharks were swimming in the oceans long before dinosaurs were roaming the land? There are hundreds of species*, big and small. Some have strange features. Look at the head of the hammerhead shark. And the wobbegong looks like a bit of carpet lying on the sea floor!"

Great white shark

Hammerhead shark

Cookiecutter shark

Wobbegong shark

"Some people think that sharks are scary, but sharks rarely hurt us. We should think of them as friends because they keep our oceans healthy."

"Sharks are apex predators*, meaning they are at the top of their food chain. They eat other animals but don't get eaten, except by larger sharks or orcas (killer whales). Sharks keep things in balance so there is enough food for everyone."

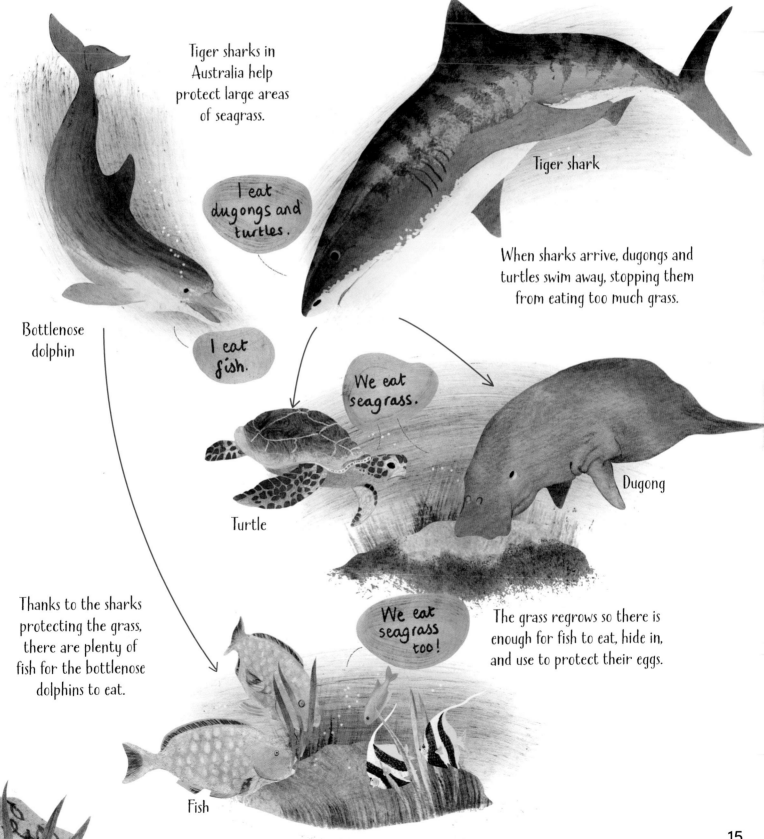

Tiger sharks in Australia help protect large areas of seagrass.

I eat dugongs and turtles.

Tiger shark

When sharks arrive, dugongs and turtles swim away, stopping them from eating too much grass.

I eat fish.

We eat seagrass.

Bottlenose dolphin

Turtle

Dugong

Thanks to the sharks protecting the grass, there are plenty of fish for the bottlenose dolphins to eat.

We eat seagrass too!

The grass regrows so there is enough for fish to eat, hide in, and use to protect their eggs.

Fish

"A shark isn't fussy about its food.
If the population* of one species is low,
sharks will hunt another species. This keeps
a balance in the ocean. Sharks also eat
old and sick animals, so they keep
populations healthy."

"Not only that," said Seb, "but where there are sharks, there is more diversity*, meaning more types of fish."

Coral reefs are like underwater cities—home to many sea creatures. Sharks patrol the reefs, looking for tasty animals to eat.

Groupers, like this one, eat smaller fish. Without sharks eating the groupers, there would be more of them and fewer small fish.

The small fish eat algae, small plants, and plant-like creatures that live on the reef. If they didn't, the algae could smother the coral and these amazing fish cities would die.

"You see!" said Seb. "Sharks are awesome and keep our oceans healthy." Everyone thought sharks were cool, but then Kai got up to speak . . .

BEAVERS

"Beavers," Kai said, "are one of nature's engineers*. They build dams to create ponds around their homes, just like kings and queens used to build moats around their castles. When beavers build their homes, they create perfect places for other animals to live too."

A beaver's home is called a lodge. It is made of sticks, logs, rocks, and mud.

Secret underwater entrances

Beavers build the dam before their lodge, so the entrances are hidden underwater.

"Beavers use their big front teeth like saws to bring down trees for their dams. This allows sunlight to reach the water where it was shaded, causing an explosion of life."

Plants and other pond life begin to grow in the water, and tiny creatures hatch, providing food for fish and other animals.

Beaver ponds attract amphibians, such as frogs and toads. These animals mostly live on land but lay their eggs in the water.

Water birds such as herons, geese, and ducks arrive because there is so much food.

"The beavers create habitats* for new food webs," explained Kai.

"Beavers were creating these watery landscapes when mammoths and saber-toothed tigers roamed the land. Beavers are rodents, like rats and guinea pigs, but they have adapted to become strong swimmers."

Beavers can close their ears and nostrils.

They have thick, waterproof fur.

They have huge, orange front teeth.

They use their tails to steer when swimming, for support when standing up, and to warn others if danger is near.

Their front feet are like hands—good for gripping and carrying.

Their back feet are webbed, like flippers.

"Beavers are experts at creating wetlands.
Their dams trap rainwater and melted snow."

Beavers cut down up to 300 trees
a year, but when they run out
of good trees, they move on,
allowing new trees to grow.

Beavers make their ponds deeper by carving
out channels underwater to swim from pond
to pond. This means the ponds rarely dry up.

Beaver dams act like filters, cleaning
the rivers as they run downstream
and spreading the water wider.
Lots of clean water means lots
of fish, so plenty for bears to eat.

"Brilliant beavers!" the class agreed, but then Otto got
up to tell everyone about his important animal ...

BATS

"My aunty is a bat scientist," said Otto. "We've been out in the dark to watch them. Most bats eat insects, but some eat fruit, nectar, and seeds. They all have superpowers! Insect-eating bats SEE using sound. It helps them navigate in the dark and hunt for food."

This skill is called echolocation. The bats make really high-pitched sounds that echo back to them. Their brains build up a picture of what is in front of them. If it is an insect, bats can tell how fast it's moving and in which direction.

"Bats are both night predators* and pollinators.
They play a part in bringing us some of the
most delicious foods we eat."

POLLINATORS
Fruit bats pollinate
more than 500 species
of flowering plants,
including bananas.

NIGHT
PREDATORS
Chocolate is made
from cocoa beans
from the cocoa
tree. Without bats,
we would lose a lot
of the beans to
hungry insects.

SEED DISPERSERS*
Fruit bats spread seeds in their poo
as they fly, so new plants, like vanilla
orchids, grow in other areas of forest.

"Bananas, vanilla, and chocolate! Thank you, bats!"

"A bat's other superpower is being able to fly.
Bats are mammals, like humans, but no
other mammal can fly."

Look under this bat's wing.
Can you see what looks like
an arm and a hand?

What do you think
its face looks like?

This claw is a bat's thumb.
The bat uses it to climb trees.

The bat's wing is a piece of
skin that stretches from
its arm to its foot.

Unlike birds, bats have flexible, folding wings.
This makes them night-flying acrobats.
Bats can change direction in a split-second
as they chase insects.

"Another incredible thing about insect-eating bats is
that they hunt at night in huge numbers."

Bats eat thousands
of insects, including
mosquitoes. That's
good for people in
countries where
mosquitoes carry
disease.

Keeping insect populations down helps cotton farmers too.
Bats reduce the need for pesticides, which saves the
farmers money but is also good for our planet.

By studying bats' superpowers,
scientists have developed amazing
technologies, such as ultrasound
to see inside people's bodies.

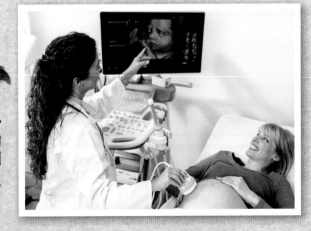

"Bats are amazing," said Otto. Myra agreed, but she wanted to
switch the conversation from awesome bats to magnificent cats...

TIGERS

"Did you know that no two tigers look the same?" asked Myra. "Every tiger has unique stripes, which helps scientists count and track them. Scientists have to do this because there are only around 4,500 tigers left in the wild."

Tigers live across Asia, from India to Siberia. The smallest is the Sumatran tiger. It is one of the rarest big cats, with only 400 left living wild on the island of Sumatra in Indonesia.

"A hundred years ago, Sumatra was covered with lush rain forests full of animals. Thousands of tigers kept everything in balance."

The tigers were apex predators in their own bit of this vast jungle. They would roam their territory looking for prey*, protecting their territory from other tigers and keeping populations in check.

Save the tigers

Today, large areas of forest have been cleared and turned into farms or cities. Sumatran tigers, rhinos, elephants, orangutans, and sun bears are now endangered* because they have less space to live in.

"Many people, from presidents to princes, charities to children, are trying to protect these animals and what is left of their rain forest habitats."

"But here's the good news!" said Myra, showing her photos. "In India, the number of tigers doubled after the tiger was protected and made the national animal of India."

"There are special tiger reserves across India where tigers are free to roam and breed and raise their cubs."

Protecting tiger habitats means protecting the trees, plants, and animals that live there, including this endangered orangutan.

Tigers love the water and are good swimmers. This helps them cool down in hot weather.

Tigers live alone, except when a female has cubs. She usually has two or three, and they stay with her until they are about two years old. Wild tiger cubs are a hopeful sign that numbers are increasing.

"If we don't protect tigers, they could become extinct like dinosaurs," Myra said. "So for me, the tiger is the most important animal of all."
Grace got up, worried that her animal might not seem as exciting as a tiger ...

29

KRILL

"You've probably never heard of krill, and you haven't seen them in the zoo," said Grace, "but without them, many whales would have nothing to eat."

Antarctic krill are tiny shrimp-like creatures that form huge swarms in the ocean. Whales scoop them up in their mouths.

Blue whales and humpback whales travel to Antarctica to feast on krill. They eat millions of them, but there are billions left.

"Krill are at the heart of the entire Antarctic food web. Penguins, seals, fish, and birds all eat krill. Antarctic animals that don't eat krill eat something else that does."

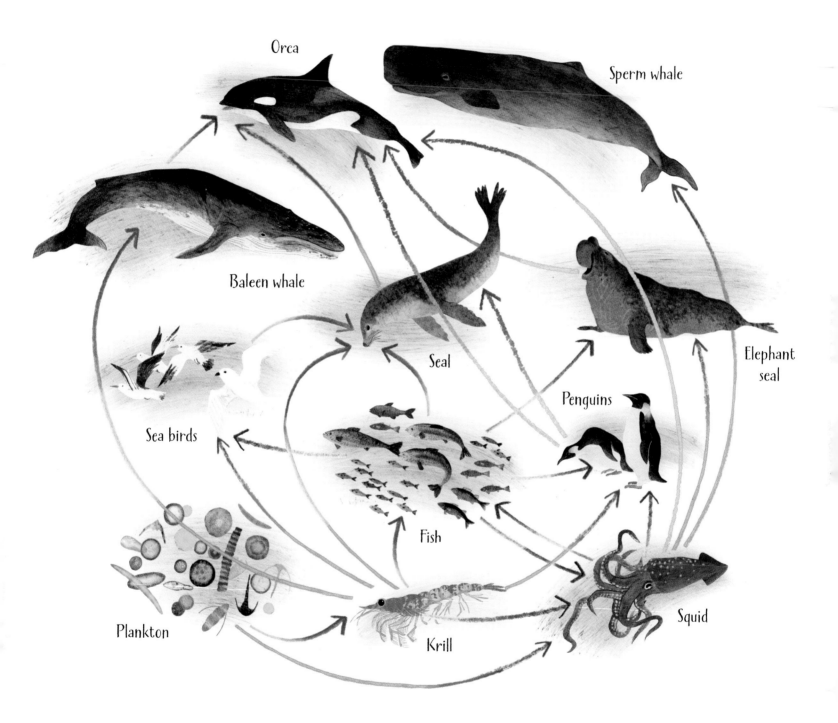

"Blue whales and humpback whales are baleen whales. They have baleen in their mouths instead of teeth. Baleen works like a sieve, filtering out the krill from the water so whales can eat them."

Grace showed her photos.
"This is an Antarctic krill," she said.
"It's like a tiny see-through shrimp,
and it's the size of your thumb."

A krill can live for
10 years. You can
tell its age by the
size of its eyes.

See-through
body covered
by a thin shell

Feeding legs

Gills

Swimming
legs

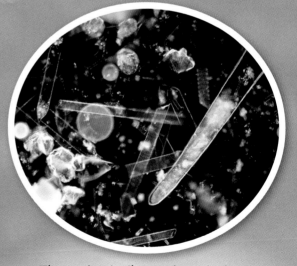

This is what krill eat—phytoplankton.
These tiny plant-like things are
very nourishing.

The whale shark is the biggest fish in the ocean, but it eats krill and plankton. It doesn't have teeth, so it swims through swarms with its mouth wide open.

These little pink creatures are lobster krill. Their swarms can be so big they can be seen from space!

Large penguins enjoy a fish meal, but little ones, like this gentoo and its chick, eat krill.

"Because so many ocean creatures depend on krill, the krill must be the most important animal of all."

The class was silent. Could something they had never heard of be THAT important?

Their teacher congratulated the children on their wonderful presentations and gave them all an Animal Champion badge.

"So who is right?" George asked.

beaver

elephant

"Look at them," said their teacher, pointing to photos on the wall.
"They are ALL important. Can you imagine a world without them?"

ANIMAL of the

bee

ti

shark

krill

"So, let's vote. Which do YOU think is
the most important animal of all?"

KEYSTONE SPECIES

All the animals in this book are known as keystone species*, meaning that many plants and animals where they live depend on them. Here are some more. Maybe you would like to be their Animal Champion?

WOLVES
Wolves are apex predators in some mountain and forest habitats. They keep populations of other species (such as deer) in check, benefiting all the wildlife.

SEA OTTERS
Sea otters eat sea urchins—prickly animals that eat kelp forests. These seaweed forests provide homes and food for many marine animals.

CORALS
Corals are living creatures that create coral reefs. These reefs provide homes, food, and shelter for thousands of other animals.

SEA STARS
Sea stars are predators that feed on mussels and shelled creatures that other animals can't eat. If the sea stars didn't eat them, they could take over the ecosystem*.

EFFECTS ON ECOSYSTEMS

An ecosystem is a place where a group of living things, including plants, mammals, birds, insects, and humans, live and interact with one another. It can be as big as a rain forest or as small as a rock pool. Everything is connected, and what one species eats or how it behaves affects other species.

BROWN BEARS AND GRIZZLY BEARS
Bears are predators, seed dispersers, and ecosystem engineers. They help enrich the soil when they dig for roots and rodents.

HUMMINGBIRDS
Hummingbirds are important to many tropical plants because they pollinate the flowers with their long beaks and tongues.

EARTHWORMS
Earthworms provide food for birds and other small animals. They also enrich the soil by breaking down dead plants and roots, which helps new plants grow.

PRAIRIE DOGS
Prairie dogs create habitats for other creatures by digging out networks of burrows and enriching the soil. They are also food for predators.

FIND OUT MORE

Now that you know how special these animals are, you should know that humans are doing things that affect them. If you care about animals, here is more information . . .

ELEPHANTS
Landscape engineers and seed dispersers

People are the biggest threat to elephants in both Africa and Asia. They turn elephant habitats into farms and cities. Poachers kill African elephants for their meat and tusks.

LEARN MORE AT
National Geographic Kids,
www.natgeokids.com

Save the Elephants, www.savetheelephants.org

BEES
The world's pollinators

Bees pollinate many of the plants that produce fruits, vegetables, and nuts. They are under serious threat from the loss of wildflower meadows, disease, large-scale farming, and the spraying of pesticides.

LEARN MORE AT
Bee Conservancy,
www.thebeeconservancy.org

Xerces Society, www.xerces.org

SHARKS
Apex predators

Sharks are threatened by fishing. They can be caught and killed by accident in nets, but some people catch them for their fins—shark-fin soup is popular in some Asian countries.

LEARN MORE AT
Oceana, www.oceana.org

Shark Research Institute,
www.sharks.org/kids-helping-sharks

BEAVERS
Ecosystem engineers

Beaver populations declined because they were hunted for their fur. They are making a comeback today, thanks to positive action by conservationists.

LEARN MORE AT
Beaver Institute,
www.beaverinstitute.org

Canadian Geographic,
www.canadiangeographic.ca

BATS
Predators, pollinators, and seed dispersers

There are more than 1,400 bat species living all around the world, but 200 species in more than 60 countries are endangered, mostly because their habitats are disappearing.

LEARN MORE AT
National Wildlife Foundation
www.nwf.org

Bat Conservation* International,
www.batcon.org

TIGERS
Apex predators

Wild tiger numbers have decreased by 95% in a century. Some subspecies are now extinct. International organizations have come together to try to double their numbers.

LEARN MORE AT
Fauna & Flora International,
www.fauna-flora.org

World Wildlife Fund, www.worldwildlife.org

Save the tigers

KRILL
Keystone prey

Krill are a keystone species in many of the world's oceans. In Antarctica, their numbers have reduced due to global warming and ice loss. Scientists worry this will affect the whole ecosystem.

LEARN MORE AT
National Ocean Service,
https://oceanservice.noaa.gov

Cool Antarctica, www.coolantarctica.com

GLOSSARY

Apex predators
Predators at the very top of the food chain that have no natural predators themselves

Conservation
Protecting and restoring nature and wildlife

Diversity
A measure of the wide range and variety of different species

Ecosystem
All the animals, plants, and living things together in one place

Endangered
In danger of becoming extinct

Engineer
A person or animal that designs, builds, and maintains buildings, machines, or structures, including natural habitats

Evolved
Changed in a very small way, over time, from one generation to the next (from parent to children)

Habitat
A place that is the natural home for an animal or plant

Keystone species
An animal, plant, or other living thing that has a very large effect on the place and wildlife where it lives

Pollinator
An animal that transfers pollen from one plant to another

Population
The number of any single species in one place (for example, in a woodland, a country, or in total around the world)

Predator
An animal that hunts or catches and eats other animals

Prey
An animal that is hunted, killed, and eaten by a predator

Seed disperser
An animal that spreads seeds, often by eating fruits and dropping the seeds in their poo

Species
A specific type of animal (or other living thing) that shares characteristics but is different from another type of animal. For example, African and Asian elephants are very similar, but they have a number of particular differences that make them two separate species of elephant.

INDEX

PHOTO CREDITS

SHUTTERSTOCK.COM: Page 8 Asian elephant © SasinTipchai; **9** San bushman © Silvia Truessel, germination © JAAOJA, dung beetle © Michael Sheehan; **12** honeybee © Melinda Nagy; **13** beekeeper © EsfilPla; swarm on honeycomb © Poring Studio; dusky langur © Sanit Fuangnakhon; **16** baby shark © mycamerawork; **17** coral reef © frantisekhojdysz, Nassau grouper © RLS Photo, green algae © Rich Carey; **20** North American beaver © Jody Ann; **21** beaver cutting a tree © Procy, beaver dam © O Brasil que poucos conhecem, brown bear © BlueBarronPhoto; **24** bat flying © Independent birds; **25** bats at sunset © imo, cotton picker in Brazil © Alf Ribeiro, ultrasound scan © hedgehog94; **28** Indian tiger © Ondrej Prosicky; **29** tiger and cub © Julian W, Siberian tiger © Martin Mecnarowski, Sumatran orangutan © Don Mammoser; **32** Antarctic krill © Tarpan; **33** whale shark © Onusa Putapitak, lobster krill ©Apple Pho, gentoo penguins © Adel Korkor Photography; **36** wolf © Vlada Cech, sea otter © rbrown10, coral reef © Mike Workman, ochre starfish © Darren J. Bradley; **37** brown bear and cubs © ArCaLu, fiery-throated hummingbirds © Ondrej Prosicky, common earthworm © Mama Belle and the kids, prairie dog © MyImages - Micha. **ISTOCKPHOTO.COM: Page 32** Marine plankton © tonaquatic.